TO
DAN, SAM + SPE[...]
EMPATHY & KINDNESS WIN.

The Student Loan Debt Solution

A New American Paradigm

Rory Curtis

To Lee Ann,

whose empathy and kindness know no boundaries.

Table of Contents

Author's Note v

Introduction vii

The Business of Empathy 10

The Numbers 23

The Need for Empathy 28

The Shift 33

The Impact 39

Leaving a Legacy 44

The Paradigm Circles 48

Implementation 54

The Urgency of a New Paradigm 62

The Impact on Abortion 66

$30 Trillion in Debt 70

A Cure Instead of an Aspirin 75

Politics and the Paradigm 79

The 1.5 Page Solution 85

Chapter 16 89

What Next? 89

Acknowledgements 91

About the Author 92

References 99

Author's Note

I recently turned 65 years old and am at the age of reflection. I am at the point in a person's life where there is a great deal of calmness. I have met the everyday challenges in life that Americans often deal with, and I have confidence that I can get through the remainder of my time here on earth without a great deal of worry. At the same time though, the age of reflection brings with it a sense of urgency. I realize that while I am not ready to call it quits, time is not on my side anymore. This short book is my legacy that I leave to the millions of Americans who know in their hearts that our country can be so much better.

-Rory Curtis

"If you're going to live, leave a legacy. Make a mark on the world that can't be erased."

-Maya Angelou

Introduction

Imagine a new America, not that different from the old one, but less narcissistic. It would be an America that values things like empathy and love, just as much as money and power. A new positive thought process would be embraced and a shift in the American paradigm would begin to emerge. The old patterns of thinking would be replaced by newer and more empathetic ones. America would graduate from the computer age and subsequently enter the beginning of the age of kindness. Hundreds of millions of Americans would work together to solve some of America's biggest problems. Hunger, homelessness, illiteracy, crime, abortion, racism, and others would all be impacted beyond measure, and generation after generation would gradually work to solve these issues almost completely. Eventually, special government programs to solve these problems would be nearly non-existent, because there would be almost no need for them anymore. There would be no national debt and America would have a balanced and manageable budget. Taxes would be lowered because there would be no need for what would only be considered a surplus of money.

While this kind of promised land scenario might seem as if it came from a work of science-fiction, what if I told you that it could be done with only a couple of minor changes in the American educational system?

I am not a scholar, an educator, a constitutionalist, a statistician, or a psychologist, and I am certainly not a politician. I do not have a degree from Harvard, Yale, or for that matter, a degree at all. In some ways this makes it easier to voice my thoughts and opinions openly and unapologetically without outside interference.

Understanding the premise of this book does not require a degree, a job title, a label, a political affiliation, or a particular religion. You do not have to be a democrat or a republican. What gender you identify as does not matter. What it will require is an open mind, a big heart, and empathy for others.

You will not find in this book a saturation of statistics, referenced psychological opinions from so-called experts, or biblical quotes. This book is far too simple to require them. Statistics can be twisted, and psychologists don't always agree, so why include anything except inarguable facts?

What you will find in this book is my concept called The Great American Paradigm Shift. It is an easy-to-understand, common sense plan to make America exponentially smarter, kinder, richer, and more tolerant for generations to come, and at the same time, solves America's $2 trillion student debt problem.

Chapter I

The Business of Empathy

My concerns over student debt have nothing to do with me having taken out a loan. I have never borrowed money for education. Also, chasing a degree at this time is not as important to me as perhaps it once was. So, why would I be concerned about someone else's debt and education? Because $2 trillion worth of student loan debt affects every single one of us. That kind of debt chokes the economy, causes downturns in home sales, slows construction, and causes the unemployment rate to go up. Yes, I am affected by outstanding student loans, just as you are too.

When you begin to realize that a problem affects you, your family, and everyone else, you start looking for answers. That is the first step, and when you finally exhaust all manners of solutions created by your own way of thinking, there is a chance you might take another step called 'intellectual humility". It's the act of admitting that maybe you might be a little bit wrong, and don't have the solutions you think you did.

My mind works a little differently. I attack problem-solving backwards from most. I see things from a unique perspective where kindness and empathy should prevail above business plans and profitability. Kindness and empathy are their own rewards, but they can also be profitable. There is no better business strategy than the one that puts its self-interests aside and focuses on the needs of others. I start out in step two and generally bypass step one altogether.

In my business, I used to give away merchandise to every charitable organization that came into my store asking for a donation. My business model could have limited donations to one specific charitable group, but it seemed rather arrogant for me to decide which entity was the most deserving. Would we support cancer research, veterans, churches, schools, or homes for the homeless? Who am I to make that decision? In the end the only conclusion we could come to was to support everyone that asked for our help, even if it was in the smallest of ways, and touch as many lives in our community as possible. At the end of our first year in business, we were nearly bankrupt.

It would have been easy to stop donating to charity, but that would have only fixed my personal financial situation, and these charities would suffer. My way of thinking was that instead of giving less to charity, I would *and should*, give more. Like I said before, I tend to think backwards from most, and to most business owners this would be a difficult concept to understand.

Imagine at a company board meeting, your Chief Financial Officer says the company is giving away too much money and facing bankruptcy. Then you stand up and tell the board that the problem would be fixed if we stepped up as a company, doubled down, made charitable donations an integral part of our business model, and increased our donations by 1900%. Well, luckily we did not have to answer corporate board members, so we were able, with some creative and out-of-the-box thinking, able to pull it off.

We took a hard look at our strategy of giving away $20 worth of merchandise to five hundred charitable groups in our first year in business. The premise was that five hundred organizations could then use those twenty dollars' worth of merchandise for silent auctions and fundraising events and that we could impact five hundred groups instead of only a few.

One of the big problems we soon found was that we had no idea what our return was on our investment. There was no tangible way to track it. We had no idea if anyone from the bulk of these groups ever returned the favor and came back into our store to shop. To be fair though, why would they? Did we help anyone with a $20 donation? What had seemed like a great concept at its inception proved to be either a dismal failure, or a success that we had no way of proving. For a concept to be a success without being able to prove it, is a business strategist's worst nightmare. It gives you nothing to double down on and you start to second guess where your financial strengths are.

We had suddenly found ourselves in the same predicament that the federal government is often in when giving away grant money. How do they know that they made a worthwhile investment, and what exactly was their return? The only difference between my little company and the federal government was that I was dealing in thousands of dollars, and the government is dealing in trillions. I suppose you could call my decision reckless to give away thousands of dollars without a way to efficiently track my returns, but what do you call it when government spending is in the trillions?

So, we came to a decision. Instead of giving groups $20 worth of merchandise to five hundred charitable groups for an annual impact of $10k, we produced an entirely different plan. We would now give them something of value to the tune of $400, worth an annual charitable impact of up to $200k. Each charitable entity would receive a gift certificate valued at $400 to be used for a wine tasting party, to be held at our store, for up to twenty guests. The charity would auction off the party to the highest bidder at one of their events. The buyer would then come into our store with up to twenty friends, where we would entertain them, tasting a little wine, preparing them a little food, and having a wonderful time. The charity benefited, and so did our business. Every time we held one of these charitable parties, it brought up to twenty new people into our store, and we were able to turn many of them into life-long customers. This strategy turned out to be so successful and so well liked by everyone involved that we at times would do this over one hundred times per year. By solving the problem of how to give more money to charity instead of less, our business has become more profitable. Every school, hospital, church, and charitable group that we touched became a little more successful. The result was that of a team relationship. The charities, their supporters, and our business worked together towards a common cause, enriching the lives of several thousand people in our local community. What does this have to do with education? Because by using a similar strategy, Americans could free themselves from student loans and at the same time, enrich the lives of millions.

Because of this changeup of strategy, we were also able to track our success, unlike the old business plan of throwing donations to the wind, hoping that we would see some return. Instead, we could see an actual reward for our investment. Eventually, after we had done these tasting parties for a while, we were able to produce some startling statistics and it changed forever how we would advertise in the future. We looked at charitable donations differently. No longer would donations be a burden, a hardship, or part of an unproven business concept. It would instead become an integral part of our business where we would seek out charitable groups that we could make more donations to. In short, helping people accomplish what was important to them benefited our business.

We began to make a comparison of our charitable gifts to various investments we had made in business advertising. We would look at a receipt where we had spent hundreds of dollars on a specific magazine ad and then try to determine how many people came into our store because of that ad. We then looked at a tasting party where we had spent far less money and then saw up to twenty new customers come into our store. Our cost per new customer in our store from the magazine ad was impossible to determine. The cost of attracting a new customer by focusing on charitable giving turned out to be almost nothing because while they were in our store, they spent money.

There was no contract between our business and the charities that we helped, but instead a collaboration was formed that benefited everyone. To be clear, there were no expectations on either side from our donation.

Some might say that we were not as a business donating anything because it was all tax deductible. First, none of it was deductible. I wish it were, but that is not how tax deductions work. Second, even if it was, you need to be profitable before you can show the benefits of tax deductions. We simply assisted churches, schools, hospitals, and others, by giving them something of value that they could sell at one of their events. Little did we know in the beginning that the real profit from all of this was not the financial bottom line. It was in the empathy and camaraderie that we established within our community. While advertising through traditional avenues like print, radio, and television, can work for short-term results, we established business relationships within our circle that would last for years to come.

Not all business-related empathy is as calculated or strategic as the restructuring of our business model and our donations to charity. Sometimes empathy is just about respect and things just seem to work out.

I remember a story about my grandfather. How much truth there is to the story, I don't know. There were times in my life when I thought I would research it factually, but why risk such a great tale just because it may have been a little romanticized over the years? It seems that my grandfather was a bit of a genius who never attended college. Instead of choosing a formal education, he instead traveled halfway across America to marry his high school sweetheart who had moved to California with her parents. Not long after he took a job doing menial tasks at an FM radio station. Eventually he became a radio DJ. This was before television. FM radio was king. The music of the day was Dixieland Jazz, and my grandfather had a Dixieland radio show for many years, even after he became the General Manager of the station. All good things must end though and as time went on, television started to take over. Rock and roll became the name of the game and Dixieland musicians were replaced by names like Elvis Presley and Jerry Lee Lewis. Suddenly, the coronet, clarinet, and trombone musicians of old could no longer find jobs playing the music they loved. My grandfather though, never gave up on them and continued with a weekly Dixieland radio show, promoting these great musicians every week, finding places for them to play whenever he could.

This is where the story starts to change. Reportedly, the owners of the radio station that my grandfather managed, also owned the Los Angeles Lakers. The Lakers basketball team was not the billion-dollar franchise they are today. But they were still popular enough to get my grandfather invited to some dinners and parties that included some influential people. One of these people was a guy named Walt Disney. I would have loved to have heard the conversation between my grandfather and Mr. Disney, it must have gone well. By the end of the conversation, my grandfather had been hired as a talent scout and part-time announcer for Disneyland. No longer would many of the great names in Dixieland Jazz have to flip burgers for a living.

I must have been about eight years old when I first witnessed the appreciation that these musicians had for my grandfather. I was too young to fully understand it, but I knew there was something special going on. My grandfather had invited us to a restaurant where a Dixieland band was playing. We all arrived at the same time. When we walked into the room and one of the band members recognized my grandfather, the band stopped playing in the middle of a tune and stood up until we were escorted to a table and seated. It was the kind of show of respect that we seldom see today.

It has been said that my grandfather read an entire book every night and that he never really had an opportunity to go to college. There were no student loans back then. Instead, he formed collaborations between people. He used his talents and skills to create life-long bonds with those who also helped him along the way. It was a trade-off of services that would pay him back with more than money right up to the day of his memorial service, where some of those still living musicians stopped by to pay their respects and give him a send-off.

Fast forward a couple of generations and I would be looking for musicians to play in a small beer and wine bar that I owned. Without doing it purposefully I ended up following somewhat in my grandfather's footsteps. I started hiring musicians that played jazz, rhythm and blues, and soul. Once again, these were talented musicians that had very few places to play.

I wanted these musicians to feel how special they really were and how much I appreciated them. I wanted them to feel like the stars some of them were, even if only in my tiny bar. One way I did that was by hanging framed, autographed photos of everyone who performed. At one point we had dozens of photos across the wall and lining the staircase. Doing this helped give the bands a sense of ownership. This tiny bar was theirs. It was where they were respected and appreciated.

The little bar would become the most talked about music venue in the area. It all ended though when we had to face covid, a next-door fire, and cancer. Had it not been for the collaboration and help of one another, we would have had to also close our retail store below the bar. Those relationships we made would save our business.

"One of the most important business lessons I have learned is that if you want to become successful, look for ways to help others without expectations of reward. Then have faith that the rest will take care of itself."

-Rory Curtis

Chapter 2

The Numbers

Why does America charge Americans for knowledge? Why is college free in dozens of countries, but not in America? How come we force people to take on massive amounts of student loan debt to receive the degree of their choice? None of it makes any sense.

According to US News (Wood, 2022), a public in-state college will run you around $10,000 per year. Out-of-state public colleges will run an average of over $20,000 per year, and private schools will hit around $40,000 per year, and if you want to go to Harvard, plan on spending around $60,000 per year. This is up about 20% over the last 10 years. And, who decides what tuition cost will be? Part of the decision has to do with supply and demand, and the learning institution itself. Another part of the equation has to do with state and federal financial participation, laws, and guidelines. In other words, it is a collaboration between your chosen college and the government.

Here is how it works if you want to become a high school English teacher. First, you will need a 4-year bachelor's degree. That is going to run you around $40k at least. No worries though. Just get a student loan for $40k and you are off to the races. Do not worry about paying it back. It will only cost you a little over $300 per month over the next 15 years. When you land that lucrative teaching job the median pay rate in America is around $4,000 per month. Now subtract that $300 a month student loan payment from your $4,000 gross and you are around $14k a year above the national poverty guidelines for a family of four. You will not be eligible for food stamps because you made a little too much money and missed the window. By the time you buy a car and make your monthly payment on your student loan, your income-to-debt ratio will significantly impact the amount of home loan you will be eligible for. That is *if* a bank loans you money at all. Hopefully, you will have a 2-income household or a second source of income.

So, everybody is happy! The college made money, the federal government is making interest on your student loan, and you landed your dream job of teaching high school

English. If any of this sounds ridiculous, it is because sadly, it is. It is a convoluted mess that America should be ashamed of, and it affects over 40% of the nearly two million high school teachers in America today. Even worse, this is not limited to high school teachers. While various sources seem to produce somewhat different statistics, (possibly because the amounts are escalating so quickly), it is safe to say that over forty million Americans owe a total of around $2 trillion in student debt.

It is big business at both the government level and at the learning institution level. There are huge dollars at stake, and neither entity is anxious to excuse that kind of debt or start lowering tuitions. Any small business owner will tell you that the idea is to charge more for your product and work less. So, why would a university charge less for their products, overcrowd their classrooms, and work harder to make the same amount of money? Based on that question, it makes a defense of the learning institutions and their financial strategy. But here is a question for you. If an increased number of college courses are now taught online, lowering the cost, other than greed, why has tuition gone up 20% over the last 10 years?

The good news is that all of this is fixable. In fact, it is not only fixable, but with The Great American Paradigm Shift concept in place that $2 trillion could be paid back repeatedly in the form of a partnership and trade of services. Forty-five million Americans would not have to come out of pocket with a single dime. The entire student loan debt could be paid in full, with interest. There would be no further multi-billion-dollar forgiveness plans, and our country would be a better, kinder, happier, and more profitable place.

"Education is the most powerful weapon which you can use to change the world."

-Nelson Mandela

Chapter 3

The Need for Empathy

Teen suicide is at an all-time high. According to a recent article by UCLA Health (Cohen, 2022), suicide is the second-leading cause of death among people ages 15 to 24. Nearly 20% of high school students report serious thoughts of suicide, and 9% have tried to take their own lives. This statistic should be frightening. What it means is that if you walk into a classroom of twenty-three students, there is a good chance that five of them have had serious thoughts of ending their lives, and two of them have attempted it. To take it a step further, if in your extended family you have five members going to high school, take a hard look at them. There is a chance that one of those five family members has had serious thoughts of committing suicide.

Endhomelessness.org reports that homelessness in America is trending upward and includes over 400,000 people. About 6% of those are military veterans and 5% are under the age of twenty-five. Those who are young and homeless are often considered vulnerable to things like sex trafficking and becoming drug mules due to their age. About 50% of homeless people are White.

According to sentencingproject.org (Ashley Nellis, 2023) the U.S. prison population ranks amongst the highest in the world with over five million Americans living in prison or are under some sort of criminal supervision. Nearly two million of those people are Black.

When it comes to hunger, according to feedingamerica.org (America, 2022), thirty-four million people in the United States are food insecure. Of those over ten million are children. Fifty-three million people turned to government funded food programs in 2021, and 100% of all counties in America have food insecurity issues.

The national debt is now over $30 trillion. It has nearly doubled over the last 10 years.

According to Forbes.com (Duszynski-Goodman, 2023), 42% of U.S. adults with a diagnosable mental health condition went untreated because they could not afford the help they needed. That 42% amounts to about twenty-eight million people. Pause for a minute and think this stat through. If twenty-eight million people with mental health issues are not getting the help they need, then what are they doing and where are they doing it? Here is an example. In 2023 a group of people were riding the subway together. One person in the group was a young Black man who had previously been arrested forty times. This young Black man reportedly threatened passengers and one of those passengers was a former marine who put the young man in a choke hold, eventually ending his life. Who is at fault here? The marine? The young Black man? Or could it possibly be the fault of society in America? Maybe America dropped the ball. Maybe America should have regarded those forty arrests as forty pleas for help. Twenty-eight million people who cannot get the mental health help they need is a disgusting statistic and America should be embarrassed.

    Let us not forget veterans either. In 2020 over 6,000 of them committed suicide. Do the math. That is about one soldier who served our country committing suicide every hour and a half.

Under the present American paradigm these problems are not going away. Americans know this, but instead of looking for solutions and managing them with empathy, we for the most part turn our heads away and callously ignore the issues. It is an ugly way of dealing with some very real conditions, but it has now become habitual. Something needs to change. We need to establish new healthy ways to address American problems. We need to break the cycle. We need to establish a different pattern, a new paradigm, a paradigm that includes common financial sense and reignites empathy in America.

"Nobody cares how much you know until they know how much you care."

-Theodore Roosevelt

Chapter 4

The Shift

It is time to pay off student debt. While it would be nice if education were free to everyone, debt forgiveness of $2 trillion is just about as ludicrous as the current paradigm in America. It is also safe to assume that we cannot expect forty-five million Americans to produce that kind of money any time soon, if ever.

President Joe Biden, a democrat, recently introduced a plan of forgiveness that would have eliminated up to $20,000 in debt per person who owed money on student loans. Critics of the plan cried foul. Their grievances voiced concern of taxpayers with no student loan debt being forced to foot the bill for $430 billion. While this plan gave many Americans optimism, a republican leaning U.S. Supreme Court ruled against the plan.

Regardless, the debt needs to be paid. The Biden plan of forgiveness would have only accounted for a fraction of the total debt. It was at best an aspirin that would have to be given repeatedly, and not the cure that America deserves.

So, how do we satisfy people on both sides of the fence, both republicans and democrats? The answer is in creating a fresh and sensible bipartisan plan that will permanently solve the problems associated with student loans. Instead of Americans being buried in $1.5 trillion worth of debt that might never be paid, a new affordable type of currency would be created.

People with student debt are generally not deadbeats. They do not avoid paying off their debt on purpose. They just do not have the available income. But, while they may be short on cash, they do have a couple of things of value that the government wants. Because of their education they now have knowledge and skills that can benefit others, and the government needs those skills that they have loaned money on, in the worst conceivable way.

Think of student debt from a business owner's perspective. One day your accountant has a meeting with you and says that the money in your accounts receivable category has exploded to the tune of half a trillion dollars. While that might be great news if everyone paid you, that is not always the case and at best, it will take you years to get it back, if ever. Your accountant goes on and explains your options. First, you could spend your own time and money and be more aggressive in collecting payments on those overdue accounts. Another option would be to hire a collection agency. Both options require an expenditure, whittling away at your bottom line. But then your_accountant produces a third option. It would be an option where people who owed you money could give you something more valuable than the cash they owe you. They instead would give you their professional knowledge and skills to help solve some of your business's biggest problems. Their expertise could be used to promote your business through social media, help your expansion, hire better staff, find money through grants, or maybe just by saving a couple hundred dollars per month because one of the people who owe you money owns a landscaping business. He and his staff can take your place behind the mower for a while. Less of your time behind a mower or doing menial tasks means you have more time to take care of the important stuff, and in turn make more money. The landscaper was going to have trouble paying you back, if ever, and you get significant value for your original investment.

Teachers know how to teach. So why not give teachers the opportunity to work a few hours a week using their skills for a charitable cause? In exchange, they would receive educational credits, which would reduce what they owe on their student loans. Let teachers do what they are trained for by tutoring and mentoring kids, helping to lower the suicide rate of young adults. Everybody wins in this scenario. Teachers reduce their debt, the government gets help with solving a tragic teen problem without throwing more money at it, and perhaps a young and beautiful student decides his or her life is worth living. The amount of debt excused on the student loan would be far less than the added costs and governmental expenditures for grants, programs, litigation, and health care. The government would be getting value for the outstanding loans and the return would be enormous, far exceeding any interest that was to be achieved by the loan.

So, how about helping to solve the problem of homeless people in America? Teachers are not the only ones with knowledge, skills, and student debt. Engineers, architects, electricians, and carpenters have some of the same qualifying attributes and challenges. So, why not put them to work hammering nails, installing light switches, and creating new and insightful ways to build shelters for the homeless?

How many people are there in the food service industry that are facing massive student loan debt would be available to spend a few hours a week working in soup kitchens?

There is something else going on here as all of this is taking place. Building shelters for the homeless, feeding the hungry, and helping our veterans is a constant reminder of what is genuinely important in this world. These acts of kindness immerse both givers and receivers in empathy.

"My religion is very simple. My religion is kindness."

— Dalai Lama XIV

Chapter 5

The Impact

So, forty-five million Americans are facing student debt amounting to $2 trillion. Many of these loans are more than 10 years old and may never be paid back but let me ask a question. If suddenly there was a windfall of money and every single student paid off their loans, taking that $2 trillion balance down to zero, where would that $2trillion that was paid go? Think about that. Would it be spent on feeding children, housing the homeless, or reducing that $30 trillion national debt? Who would decide where that money goes? Well, this much we know for sure. There is not one chance in forty-five million that the person making that decision would be you.

But here is one of the beautiful elements of The Great American Paradigm Shift. There would be no requirement for a person to participate, but if you wanted to pay off your student loan debt by working for a charity you could choose your own charity to work for.

You could pick your cause. You pick where your portion of that $2 trillion goes. The government does not tell you what charity to work for. Instead, you tell the government where you want your money to go, by working for the charity of your choice. And, unlike many government programs where diluted money trickles its way down to the end recipient, your time and effort under The New American Paradigm goes directly to your cause.

The potential impact of all of this is so great that it is difficult to wrap your head around it. It is the reverse of the negative way that we are conditioned to think about debt. Think about loans in general today and you will begin to understand what I mean. If you are late making a loan payment, you may have to pay a penalty with the money that you did not have to make the payment in the first place. Miss multiple payments and the loan company turns up the pressure. Here come the letters, phone calls, maybe a repossession, or even a foreclosure. Your credit score is ruined, and you might even end up before a judge, meanwhile you get further and further away from paying what you owe.

There is also something else very disturbing about student loans. Filing for bankruptcy will not excuse a student loan debt, except in the rarest of cases, at least not at the time of this writing. Once you sign up for a student loan, you are stuck with it forever. Predatory lenders love this. It enables them to charge huge interest rates, sometimes up to 35%. And they can in theory make this loan to anyone and everyone because they are virtually guaranteed to get their money. Young people fresh out of high school become easy prey for seasoned professional lenders who specialize in serial abuse of Americans seeking a college education.

The New American Paradigm is a unique, but more sensible, way of thinking. If you want to pay off your student loan debt here is not only a way to pay it off without penalties, but to create a positive impact on a charity that is dear to you.

Everyone should love the concept of The New American Paradigm, because at least potentially, instead of forty-five million people who owe money, we now have forty-five million people putting in a few hours a week to solve some of the worst problems in America. Homelessness, teen suicide, hunger, literacy, and more would all be directly impacted by The Great American Paradigm Shift. These are forty-five million educated people with a tremendous variety of skillsets working to solve problems that the government has not been able to. Instead of a lender-borrower relationship, a partnership of sorts would evolve that pays back student debt with interest, creates empathy, attacks problems head-on, and sets a new paradigm for America. Forty-five million participants donating 5 hours per week of their time comes out to over eleven billion empathetic person-hours every year helping America become a better place.

There is a problem with this scenario though, if you can call it a problem. What happens when all that debt is paid off, predatory lenders no longer have jobs, and student loans become outdated and obsolete?

"We cannot solve our problems with the same thinking we used when we created them."

-Albert Einstein

Chapter 6

Leaving a Legacy

Education should be easily accessible by every single American. Not one person should ever again be punished by massive financial debt in return for knowledge. The Great American Paradigm Shift essentially puts an end to it.

As a part of the paradigm, anyone who wants to receive an education can do so regardless of their financial situation without taking out a student loan of any kind. Those who want to pursue a trade school certificate, associate degree, Bachelors, or Doctorate could do so without going into debt.

Here is how it would work. Every American would be able to earn classroom hours by volunteering themselves for worthy charitable causes. For instance, if you volunteer in a soup kitchen for an hour helping to feed the poor, in return you would get a digital or computer credit for 1 hour of classroom learning. Think of it as earning yourself a scholarship, 1 hour at a time, because of your commitment to serve your country. You could volunteer for as much charitable work as you want and earn as many educational credits as you need to achieve your goals.

There is also a crucial element included in this program. That is, that parents and grandparents should be able to earn these educational credits for their kids and grandkids. The credits should be inheritable. Grandparents should be able to leave a legacy for generations to come. The credits could never be sold or used as currency, but they could, *and should*, be able to be freely given to family members and others.

Imagine America with a new empathetic paradigm where Grandma takes one of her grandkids with her as she delivers meals to the hungry. When is the best time to teach people the value of empathy? Well, when they are young. So, all this time, not only is grandma helping people in her community, and helping her grandchild with a future college education, she is teaching that grandchild empathy for fellow Americans. It also perhaps gives grandma a new purpose in life, doing something of value and making her own personal impact on the community.

The New Paradigm would potentially have forty-five million people paying off their student loans, using their skills for charity, and creating a pattern of empathy for generations to come.

"The biggest deficit that we have in our society and in the world right now is an empathy deficit. We are in great need of people being able to stand in somebody else's shoes and see the world through their eyes."

-President Barack Obama

Chapter 7

The Paradigm Circles

There is a bit of a phenomenon that happens when you give freely to charitable causes without expectations of anything in return. Somehow, some way, those acts of empathy towards others and good faith seem to find their way back to you. Every time you do something good for someone without expectations of something in return, you start creating a circle around you. Call this circle an aura or good karma if you want. It is not a new concept. For those whose religion considers it to be a form of tithing, the concept is older than the bible itself.

As you do more for people and put others' needs before yourself your circle becomes larger and larger. Eventually your circle starts to overlap with the good karma circles of others and some magic begins. Little miracles begin to happen. These circles create a pattern of empathy. Your life starts to change. The lives of other people begin to change. Soon your circle will intersect with many others, and empathy will no longer be something you think about. It will just become a part of your everyday life.

Some years ago, we found ourselves struggling. I had lost my job. My fiancé lost her job. Her father passed away, and then my fiancé was diagnosed with cancer. It all happened within the same 30 days, and we were forced to make some life-changing decisions. We moved out of our 4-bedroom house and into one of the bedrooms of the house where her mom lived. We put a few things in storage and sold the rest. It was during this time that we stumbled upon the phenomenon of paradigm circles.

I can remember sitting together on her mothers' couch one night, making the promise to each other that if we ever found our way out of the grief and financial challenges we were facing that we would give back to the community and make a concentrated effort to give to a charitable cause or two.

A few months later we started our own business and kept our promise. And, because we could not decide whose charity was more deserving, we gave a little something to every school, church, scout troop, hospital and charitable entity that asked us for help. Most of these donations were not tax deductible, and we gave them without any expectations in return. We simply gave them because we were keeping the promise that we had made to ourselves when we were at one of the lowest points in our lives.

Soon we had made friends with several people in the community and a positive paradigm circle began to grow. Our business started to flourish. Our empathy for others started to grow. Eventually we quit traditional advertising altogether. We did not need it anymore. Instead of buying magazine ads, we started investing in our community and began actively searching for ways we could help people. Pretty soon we were impacting over one hundred charitable entities a year.

I cannot tell you why these paradigm circles work, just trust me that they do. Years later, my fiancé's mother would pass away after a long bout with dementia, covid would shut down half of our business, and a second diagnosis of cancer would challenge us yet again. But this time it would be different. Hundreds of people would come out to support us. Some of them we had never met or seen before, but somehow we had managed to impact on their lives without us realizing it and they showed up to offer their help. We were given countless donations that we never asked for, flowers kept appearing at our place of business, hundreds signed the get-well-soon book, hundreds more bought just a little extra at our store and possibly thousands said a little prayer for us. We were truly humbled.

My fiancé and I are just two people in one small community who started with one tiny, good karma circle of influence. The Great American Paradigm Shift would potentially be based on forty-five million good karma circles all intersecting with each other. These are circles that would be created by people who donate their skills and knowledge to pay off their student loan debt and teach empathy to others.

Imagine an architect or engineer who has student loan debt. This engineer would spend a few hours a week designing and making plans for wheelchair ramps for those who are housebound. He gives the plans to a skilled carpenter who also donates his skills and knowledge to pay off his student debt. Then a scout troop comes into the picture. Young people from the scout troop donate their labor to help. They learn basic carpentry skills, how to follow plans, work together as a team, and most importantly, empathy. While the architect and carpenter are using their work to pay for current student loans, the scout troop is earning future credits that will be used much like a savings account or scholarship fund. Lastly, the housebound person in the wheelchair is no longer housebound. Suddenly a small and important bit of independence was gained. Watching traffic from the porch is no longer the limit of this persons' abilities. New positive karma circles within the paradigm emerge and old ones start to expand. Everybody wins. America wins, and the world wins just a little bit.

"It's not how much we give, but how much love we put into giving."

-Mother Theresa

Chapter 8

Implementation

If you are thinking now of how difficult it must be to make a plan like this a reality, in comparison to other programs it would be amazingly easy, especially now that we are using computers for nearly everything. Here are a handful of programs that require significantly more time, energy, and money.

Close to 90 years ago, in 1935, President Franklin D. Roosevelt signed into law Social Security to create a financial safety net for the elderly. Costs of the program are now in excess of $1 trillion per year.

In 1939 President Roosevelt would also start the food stamp program. A version of it still exists today and whenever the United States talks about the national debt; food stamps seem to be one of the things that in are danger of being cut.

In the summer of 1944 President Roosevelt would also sign the GI Bill, giving members of the military an easier path to higher education. Roosevelt was a busy guy.

Later in 1965 President Lyndon B. Johnson signed the law creating Medicare, and the Higher Education Act enabling lower and middle-income families to receive college educations.

In 1972 the Pell Grant was introduced to help low-income families pursue undergraduate degrees.

So, over the last one hundred years America has been able to implement several plans that required building from the ground up. The idea of The Great American Paradigm Shift is a minor change in thinking. Compared to programs that have already been enacted, like Medicare which deals with the everchanging dynamics of new drugs, supplemental insurance, Part A, Part B, Part G, hospitalization, doctor visits, and deductibles, the cost of The Great American Paradigm Shift is pocket change.

Student loan programs are already in existence. All The Great American Paradigm Shift does is implement a way in which student loans can be paid back. Much of the program if not all of it could be accomplished online with digital credits. It would reduce the cost of the program greatly and give the government a way to collect student debts that may have previously been uncollectable.

In an age where you can buy nearly anything with the tap of a debit card, creating a system of digital credits for charitable work should be simple.

"The most difficult thing is the decision to act, the rest is merely tenacity."

-Amelia Earhart

Chapter 9

The Economy and Unemployment

The Great American Paradigm Shift through trading skills and knowledge for education not only pays off student debt, but it pays it off with interest.

For those who incur copious amounts of student debt, there is a good possibility that they may spend at least the first few years after graduating getting their finances in order before they are able to buy a house.

Here is one of those indisputable facts about buying a house, especially a new one. Every time a house is purchased it puts people to work. Architects, lawyers, sheet rockers, real estate agents, roofers, general contractors, electricians, landscapers, painters, and a whole lot more, are now employed. Basically, every time a home is built, the unemployment rate ticks down a little bit. People are put to work earning money. The economy fires up because people now have money to spend. There inherently becomes a demand when homes are built. There becomes a need for washers, dryers, stoves, water heaters, lawn mowers, and a demand for manufacturing is created. In short, the building of new homes in America is largely responsible for creating a vibrant economy and creating tax dollars.

So why is it that we put the economy on hold? Why do we strap Americans with student debt and make it harder for them to buy a house when they graduate?

Here is a possible positive side effect that could take place with The Great American Paradigm Shift. When applying for a new home loan, banks require a huge amount of your personal history on the application. They want to know where you are employed and how long you have been there, how much money you make, how much debt you have so they can determine your income-to-debt-ratio, and a slew of other things before your loan can be underwritten. But what if the bank considered just two more things? What if the bank began to look at your student loan credits and past charitable work, and at your current volunteer work that you are doing to pay off your student debt? How would that affect your credit score? How would it affect your mortgage interest rate? How much more home could you afford with a lower interest rate? This is just a side effect that could take a couple of generations to show up on the radar, but once it does, there is a possibility that your kindness and empathy towards others could reduce your mortgage payment.

Think back about what could have happened if when you were a child, your grandmother was a part of The Great American Paradigm Shift. She would deliver food to hungry Americans in your hometown, and you would sit in the seat next to her. Grandma passed eventually but not before she left you a legacy of kindness, empathy, and college loan credits. Now here you are applying for a home loan thinking about how things might have been vastly different. If it were not for those car rides with grandma delivering food to the needy maybe you would not have that college degree and the house you are living in.

"It's the economy, stupid."

-James Carville

Chapter 10

The Urgency of a New Paradigm

In grade school we were led to believe that the American civil war from 1861 to 1865 started during the time of Abraham Lincoln and was based on the argument of Black slavery. Historians that look at it a little closer will often regard it as being a bit more complicated, blaming it on westward expansion, the cotton gin, economic integrity, politicians, and yes, slavery. I tend to think that it started at least 30 years earlier and that the civil war can be boiled down to one simple thing, a lack of empathy for others.

In 1829 Andrew Jackson became the seventh president of the United States. He would become the leader of the new democratic party and serve two terms that would last until 1837. If his name sounds familiar it is because we have honored him by putting his picture on the $20 bill.

Andrew Jackson was a slave owner. He once reportedly put an ad in the local paper offering a reward of $10 to anyone capturing and giving one hundred whiplashes to one of his runaway slaves. There was apparently a limit of three hundred lashes per slave.

In 1832, an order by U.S. Supreme Court Judge John Marshall made a decision that would protect Indian land. This decision would be ignored by Jackson who said, "John Marshall has made his decision: now let him enforce it." This was the beginning of The Trail of Tears. By order of President Andrew Jackson (McNamara, 2022), Indians were removed from their land and were marched 1,000 miles over 4 months, through harsh winter weather. Suffering from lack of food, shelter, dysentery, and exhaustion, thousands of them died and were buried along the way.

Empathy is not taught to others. It is absorbed by others slowly, a generation at a time. Those who exude empathy were not taught that trait, they instead were surrounded and immersed by it over several years, many times as young children. But hatred and racism can be absorbed that way too and children soak up their environment like a sponge. They hear people talk, they see how people react, and every day since the day they are born they are learning.

In the 1830s, white settlers were looking for a hero, and Andrew Jackson was a perfect fit. Jackson was a rich slave owner, an Indian fighter, and President of the United States. He led by example and gave the white settlers the un-spoken permission to own slaves and take land away from Indians calling it their own, even if it meant killing them. President Andrew Jackson gave white settlers the redemption they were looking for. Men, women and children absorbed the racism and hatred that their hero was selling, all in the name of real estate.

Andrew Jackson would be president for 8 years and the racism and hate would last long after he left office. In fact, it would last for generations. This racism and hate created a growing negative paradigm. And in 1861 we were able to qualify killing our own people in a civil war that lasted 4 years. Over 600,000 would die (Zeller, 2022)

"At our best, we practice empathy, imagining ourselves in the lives and circumstances of others. This is the bridge across our nation's deepest divisions."

-President George W. Bush

Chapter 11

The Impact on Abortion

The issue of abortion may be the absolute definitive test for intellectual humility. Abortion is a difficult subject matter at best. Far right conservatives call those on the left "Baby Killers" and the far left accuses the right of promoting the killing of unborn babies with coat hangers. Both sides are correct. Neither side will admit that their way of thinking might be even a little bit wrong, and yet, nobody has produced an answer that even remotely solves the issue.

I have hope that someday Americans and the world will come to terms with each other on how to cope with the issue of abortion. I look forward to the day when we as a country can stop the pointing of fingers and name-calling long enough to have a civil and productive meeting of the minds.

I believe, whole-heartedly that the killing of babies is tragic. I also believe that there has never been a little girl that dreamed of one day having an abortion. Both beliefs though, could be considered as the honest and genuine feelings of just about everybody in America. There is no great epiphany here, but I bring it up because we fail to see, that at least in these two ways, society is on the same page. It is a starting point for solutions.

The Great American Paradigm Shift would be a leap in a positive direction.

Let us examine the reasons a woman would consider an abortion. First, there are health concerns for the mother and for the baby. I would not expect that college credits would fix that. But secondly, women sometimes have abortions due to fear. It might be the fear of how a young girl will be able to provide for a child. How will she feed it when she can barely feed herself? How will she give it the care that it will need without insurance? How will she raise a child alone? Fear.

What happens though when society can erase some of those fears? What if America had a system in place where that young mother has some options?

There are multiple ways where The New American Paradigm could work. One way would be where strong opponents on the right who were anti-abortion, could form a charitable group that earned a pool of college credits. Those credits would be given to young girls who choose to have their baby rather than have an abortion. The girl receives an education and eventually can get a job that will pay her enough to start a family, get insurance, afford daycare, and get off food stamp or welfare programs. The girl wins, the baby wins, and the far-right wins. Federal and state government should also love this scenario because instead of this young woman needing support, she becomes a taxpayer.

An even easier scenario to solve the problem of abortion would be family members and friends coming together and doing college credit fund drives. Loved ones could get together, work as a team to earn a young woman college credit and give her and her child a lift instead of an abortion. For a young woman to know that she has people in her corner could make all the difference in the world.

These are just two ways that The New American Paradigm could be used to help reduce abortions in America. These are positive steps that bypass name calling and protests, and directly impact the problem with reasonable solutions.

"Great minds seek empathetic solutions. Anything else is just divisive."

-Rory Curtis

Chapter 12

$30 Trillion in Debt

In one-dollar bills, thirty trillion dollars would weigh around sixty billion pounds. That is also about the weight of six million elephants. $30 trillion is the amount of the American national debt, and it is growing. Political parties constantly blame each other for this ludicrous obligation of money, seemingly without any genuine concern about reducing it. Ask any politician about the national debt and they will instantly deflect and blame it on someone else.

There are several reasons why American debt is so high. One of those reasons is that we tend to address symptoms and give away aspirins on social issues instead of finding cures. For instance, America gives away food stamps instead of education.

Another problem causing increased national debt is that Americans tend to feel entitled and expect something more than the federal government is designed to give. The government was never supposed to fix everything, but voters keep pressuring politicians for increased money every year.

We need to attack debt from a different direction. Americans need to solve some of these issues on their own. Every year there is talk of eliminating social security and reducing Medicare, but why? Why would we spend so much money on special programs, that we risk the future of our retirements and the security of our children and grandchildren?

We need to think differently as a country. Yes, $30 trillion is a tremendous amount of money. But let us look at how The Great American Paradigm Shift might reduce it.

First, consider the potentially enormous workforce that could be involved in working for various charities.

Over forty-five million Americans would be able reduce their student loan debt immediately.

There are another fifteen million students in high schools across America who could possibly want to go to college and could earn credits.

Together that is a workforce of fifty million people, in just two social groups who would be donating only a few hours a week of their time to work under the plans of The Great American Paradigm Shift.

Fifty million people contributing five hours of their time per week is a billion hours per month.

The impact would be immense and practically instantaneous. Granted, these numbers would be at 100% participation by these two groups, but what if was only 10% participation? It would still come out to 1.2 billion hours per year. These numbers also do not reflect any outside charitable groups who may want to earn college credits that they can donate to benefit the homeless, pregnant teens, and low-income families, by enabling them to go to school.

Americorps.gov numbers indicate that the economic value of one hour of charitable service is equal to about $30 in economic impact value. $30 per hour would become the standard rate of exchange. While no actual money would change hands, student loan accounts would be credited on a dollar-for-dollar economic value. A billion hours per month would be worth about $360 billion per year. That is not enough to pay off the national debt, but it is enough to pay for around one third of the costs of social security, guaranteeing that it will be around for many years to come. And, because the charitable workforce behind The Great American Paradigm Shift grows every year, expenditures on government programs would be less and less, hacking away at the national debt.

And remember how all this started? It was with $2 trillion in student debt. At an economic value rate of $360 billion per year, that entire $2 trillion would be paid off in less than 6 years.

The bonus here is that Americans, with The Great American Paradigm Shift concept in place, inherently immerse themselves in empathy and kindness, working together to solve problems like homelessness, veteran and teen suicide, hunger, and illiteracy.

"Give a man a fish and you feed him for a day, teach society to fish and you feed America forever."

-Rory Curtis

Chapter 13

A Cure Instead of an Aspirin

There has been a lot of talk about ways to address America's issues with student loan debt.

One way is to forgive all student loan debt to the tune of up to around $2 trillion. The right side of the political aisle and even some of those on the left will never go for it. But the real problem with this scenario is although it would boost the economy, what happens in decades to come? What is to keep America from getting into this situation all over again? Excusing the current debt does nothing to solve the problem next year or in the next generation.

Another way would be to excuse a portion of student loans and give a few Americans some relief. Once again, politicians, and honestly, a lot of Americans do not want to give a free ride to people who took out a loan and promised to pay it back. This way of addressing the issue is probably the best "aspirin" example of them all. It is a very temporary fix at best. Even at an excuse of $20,000 per person, it still only comes out to a quarter of the total amount owed. It does nothing for future loans or the rising costs of education.

There are about twenty-three countries around the world that offer higher learning for free. The notion that America would be one of those countries anytime soon is ill-conceived. There are currently no politicians pushing that agenda. The idea would simply never even get to the floor for debate.

There has also been a good bit of conversation about a couple of lines written into law making it almost impossible to excuse student loan debt when filing for bankruptcy. Americans can file bankruptcy in issues of gambling debt, credit card debt, and just about anything else, except student loans. For some strange reason, we as a nation reserve that ability for those who have gambling addiction but not for those who have worked hard and gone to school. While many agree the law needs to be changed, who are we kidding here? Is giving those with student loan debt the option of bankruptcy the best America can do? Suffer through and make your payment, or file for bankruptcy. In what sadistic universe does it make sense to penalize Americans who are striving to make a better life?

The New American Paradigm is not an aspirin. It is a solution. It is a cure. It would give those with massive amounts of student debt a way to give back to America, pay back the money they owe, and do it with dignity. In generations to come student loans will be practically non-existent. There will be less need for them.

With student loans becoming a rarity, predatory lenders will no longer have a job and 35% interest rates will eventually disappear through obsolescence.

"In the end, you're measured not by how much you undertake but by what you finally accomplish."

-President Donald Trump

Chapter 14

Politics and the Paradigm

I noticed a sign in front of a small business one day, as I was taking a walk downtown. It was one of those A-frame chalkboard signs that you see in front of a lot of businesses. It read "Free Gift with Every Purchase." I knew the business and the woman who owned it, and I knew that her business was likely failing, and the purpose of the sign was to draw more customers into her store. She wanted to convey to people some sort of added value for coming into her store and shopping.

This woman often made claims of being in business for 40 years. Yet she lacked intellectual humility and missed the entire point. The reason for her lack of customers, and the reason her business was probably dying a slow painful death had nothing to do with added value or promises of free gifts. It had everything to do with her. One short look at the number of complaints filed by her customers to the Better Business Bureau would explain everything to anyone that inquired.

Forty years of business experience had not helped make this woman a successful entrepreneur. It had made her worse. Every year that her business survived, her personality became more toxic and narcissistic. She drove away customers due to her lack of empathy and kindness, and her failure to listen. This is a woman who was a poor fit for a career in which she had spent decades. While she might have had an array of other attributes, owning a retail business, and working with the public was not in her wheelhouse.

It works the same way with some politicians. Not only are they missing the point of why they are in office, they have been missing it for decades. Just because a politician has been in office for forty years, it does not mean that he or she is any good at it.

There is reason enough to feel sorry for the woman. While she was toxic, and her personality rubbed a lot of people the wrong way, in the end, the person she hurt the most was herself. Not so though with politicians and judges. Their actions can affect millions of Americans with a simple slogan, decision, declaration, or the signing of a single document.

In an era where many politicians believe that supporting their party is more important than supporting America, the odds of The Great American Paradigm Shift concept even getting before a congressional committee for discussion are slim. While just about everyone in the public sector should love the benefits of The Great American Paradigm Shift, there is enough toxicity and narcissism within the three branches of government to kick this program to the curb without even giving it a second look.

Many politicians seem to have forgotten the big picture of creating a better America. They instead have turned issues into partisan fights instead of bi-partisan collaborations. Look at almost any House or Senate vote and it is typically divided strictly down party lines. Politicians will say that they have solutions, but all too often the solutions only provide answers for their own specific lobbying groups, political pacts, and party promises.

The Great American Paradigm Shift concept is bipartisan. It favors practically everyone with only a few exceptions, such as predatory lenders and possibly some 40 year plus political veterans who are not looking out for America and only have their self-interests in mind. As stated before, The Great American Paradigm shift has nothing to do with acetaminophen. It is instead a plan, that if left unadulterated by politicians, would provide generational solutions to some of Americas biggest problems.

There is no American Paradigm pact siphoning money to politicians or judges. The Great American Paradigm Shift does not have a sign outside the door that reads "Free Gift with Every Purchase." It is a real solution that should not require it.

Because The New American Paradigm is so new and fresh in its thinking, it will be difficult for many politicians to accept. Both Republicans and Democrats will be out of their comfort zone, because of the bipartisan nature of the plan. They don't know how for the most part to work together. To make The New American Paradigm come to fruition, it *must* be bipartisan though. It is a requirement. It simply cannot get off the ground without bipartisan support.

This is an amazing project. It will take the collaboration of millions of Americans on both sides of the fence to pull it off. There is no billionaire throwing money at it. It will not be without its opponents such as lobbying groups for predatory lenders. There will also be those in congress who are influenced by those same lobbying groups. What The Great American Paradigm Shift has though is forty-five million people with student debt and hundreds of millions of Americans who want to solve some of the biggest problems that we face today and will continue to face for generations to come.

"I once led an elephant and a donkey to water, but they still didn't want to read the book."

-Rory Curtis

Chapter 15

The 1.5 Page Solution

Here is how the unadulterated bipartisan concept of how The New American Paradigm is designed to work. While politicians and lawyers might make this program description hundreds of pages long, here it is in about a page and a half.

1. There is no requirement for anyone to be a part of this program.

2. Under the program, those working for charity would be paid in the form of educational credits at a rate of $30 per hour. There would be no limit to the number of credits a person could earn.

3. Credits could not be sold, traded, or used as currency. They could however be freely given, willed, or inherited.

4. Credits could be used to pay off existing loan debt or used as an earned scholarship for future education.

5. Charitable entities who participate in the program would track earned hours and report them in the same way as they report employee paychecks. Those educational hours earned would show up on a paystub, much like state and federal taxes that are itemized on a paycheck.

6. Those who are earning educational credits would have an identification card, much like a social security or Medicare card. This would enable the participant to go online and check their credit status 24 hours a day or present that card information to a learning institution for payment of book costs and tuition.

7. Credits could be used for any college, university, or trade school, both public and private.

The Great American Paradigm Shift concept is a very simple no-frills program. There is not a nickels worth of temporary loan forgiveness written into this plan. This program instead offers a permanent solution. It fixes the problem very simply by offering an alternative way to pay off student loan debt.

"When the solution is simple, God is answering."

-Albert Einstein

Chapter 16

What Next?

This book was purposely written to be short enough to read with little effort and small enough to be carried with you and passed around. By keeping it short I was also able to make it cheap to print, and as affordable as possible. The idea was to make it so that multiple copies could be purchased, distributed, and read by the masses.

If you would like to express your support of The Great American Paradigm Shift concept to your congressperson, a good place to start is at Congress.gov. There you will find addresses, phone numbers, and email information about the U.S. senators and representatives for your state.

Next you can contact the White House at whitehouse.gov. where you can send a message to President Joe Biden, Vice President Kamala Harris, or one of the cabinet members. A cabinet member you may want to voice your support to is Dr. Miguel Cardona, who is the Secretary of Education.

If you would like to contact Former President Donald Trump, you may want to do it through 45office.com.

If you are a member of a union that has members with student debt you should express your support to other union members and suggest that the union distribute copies of this book to everyone affected.

If you are one of those wonderful people who are already doing charitable work, please pass the word along to your specific charity. Not only could your organization benefit from more volunteers, but you or someone you love could benefit from the educational credits that you earn.

This low-cost book is available on Amazon and the option is available for you to buy a copy and send it to someone as a gift. Give it to someone with student debt, a politician, a charitable organization, a friend, or whoever might benefit from it.

If you are a teacher or in the business of education, do what you can to make this book available to all students.

Acknowledgements

This book would not have been possible without the help and support of my fiancé, Lee Ann. She is the love of my life, and may our adventures together continue. Thank you., sweetheart.

Thank you to our customers who continued to give us their business and unwavering support through thick and thin. They remained at our side through Covid, cancer, and a fire. More than just customers, they have become our friends.

Though they both have passed, Lee Ann's mother and father, Ed and Evelyn, cannot go without credit. Much of the empathy that Lee Ann and I absorbed in life was through them. We are eternally grateful for all their kindness and support.

About the Author

Rory Curtis is an entrepreneur and resides in South Carolina with his fiancé, Lee Ann. Still holding true to their promise of over a decade ago, they continue to make giving back to their community a definitive part of their business model. As time permits he also does guest speaking and works as a consultant to other small business owners.

You can reach out to Mr. Curtis at his website: www.rorycurtis.com

"Where there is no enemy within, the enemies outside cannot hurt you."

-Winston Churchill

abortion, vii, 66, 67, 68
addiction, 76
Albert Einstein, 43, 88
America, vii, ix, 17, 23, 24, 25, 28, 29, 30, 31, 33, 34, 36, 41, 45, 52, 55, 59, 67, 68, 70, 71, 74, 75, 76, 77, 81, 82
Americorps, 72
Andrew Jackson, 62, 63, 64
architect, 51
bankruptcy, 12, 41, 76
Barack Obama, 47
Better Business Bureau, 80
biggest problems, vii, 35, 82, 83

billion, 18, 26, 33, 42, 70, 72
bipartisan, 34, 81, 82, 85
bonus, 73
Business, 10, 80
cancer, 11, 21, 49, 51, 91
carpenter, 52
charity, 11, 14, 17, 39, 41, 46, 50, 85, 90
church, 15, 50
civil war, 62, 64
collaboration, 16, 21, 23, 82
college, 17, 19, 23, 24, 25, 41, 45, 55, 60, 67, 68, 71, 72, 86
community, 11, 15, 17, 45, 49, 50, 51, 92

computer, vii, 45

concept, ix, 12, 13, 15, 25, 41, 48, 73, 81, 85, 87, 89

credit, 40, 45, 59, 68, 76, 86, 91

crime, vii

Cure, 75

deadbeats, 34

Democrats, 82

die, 65

Dixieland, 18, 19

Donald Trump, 78, 90

donations, 11, 12, 15, 17, 50, 51

Dr. Miguel Cardona, 89

economy, 10, 58, 59, 61, 75

education, 10, 15, 17, 33, 34, 41, 44, 45, 55, 58, 68, 70, 76, 86, 90

Elvis Presley, 18

empathy, ii, vii, viii, 11, 17, 31, 37, 42, 45, 46, 47, 48, 49, 50, 51, 52, 60, 62, 63, 65, 73, 80, 91

entrepreneur, 80, 92

food stamps, 24, 54, 70

GI Bill, 54

government, vii, 13, 23, 24, 25, 29, 34, 36, 40, 42, 56, 68, 70, 73, 81

grandfather, 17, 18, 19, 20

homelessness, vii, 28, 73

Hunger, vii

illiteracy, vii, 73

income-to-debt-ratio, 59

Indians, 63, 64

intellectual humility, 10, 66, 79

investment, 13, 15, 36

Jerry Lee Lewis, 18

Joe Biden, 33, 89

John Marshall, 63

judge, 40

Kamala Harris, 89

karma, 48, 51, 52

kindness, ii, vii, 11, 37, 38, 60, 73, 80, 91

Lee Ann, ii, 91, 92

Los Angeles Lakers, 18

manufacturing, 59

Maya Angelou, vi

Medicare, 55, 71, 86

mental health, 29

millions, v, vii, 15, 80, 82

money, vii, 10, 12, 13, 14, 16, 20, 24, 25, 33, 34, 36, 39, 40, 41, 54, 58, 59, 70, 71, 72, 77, 82, 83

narcissism, 81

national debt, vii, 29, 39, 54, 70, 72

paradigm, vii, 30, 33, 42, 44, 45, 49, 50, 52, 64

partnership, 26, 42

Pell Grant, 55

politicians, 62, 71, 75, 76, 80, 81, 82, 85

poverty, 24

predatory lenders, 42, 77, 81, 83

profit, 17

program, 45, 54, 55, 81, 85, 86, 87

racism, vii, 63, 64

real estate, 58, 64

Republicans, 82

requirement, 39, 82, 85

Rory Curtis, v, 22, 69, 74, 84, 92

school, 15, 17, 23, 24, 28, 41, 44, 50, 62, 72, 76, 86

scout, 19, 50, 52

self-interests, 11, 82

Social Security, 54

solution, 77, 82, 87, 88

solve, vii, 34, 35, 36, 41, 43, 68, 71, 73, 75, 83

statistic, 28, 30

strategy, 11, 12, 14, 15, 25

student loan, 10, 23, 24, 26, 33, 36, 37, 39, 41, 44, 51, 59, 71, 72, 75, 76, 87

suicide, 28, 30, 36, 41, 73

support, 11, 51, 68, 82, 89, 90, 91

Taxes, viii

teacher, 23, 90

temporary fix, 75

tithing, 48

toxic, 80

Trail of Tears, 63
trillion, ix, 10, 25, 26, 29, 33, 34, 39, 40, 54, 70, 71, 73, 75
US News, 23

veterans, 11, 28, 30, 37, 82
Walt Disney, 19
welfare, 68

References

America, F. (2022). *Hunger in America.* feedingamerica.org.

Ashley Nellis, P. (2023). *Mass Incarceration Trends.* sentencingproject.org.

Cohen, S. (2022, March 15). Suicide rate highest among teens and young adults. *UCLA.org*, p. 2.

Duszynski-Goodman, L. (2023). *Mental Health Statistics.* Forbes HEALTH.

McNamara, R. (2022). *American Indian Removal Policy and the Trail of Tears.* thoughtco.com.

Wood, E. K. (2022). See the Average College Tuition in 2022-23. *U.s. News*, 1.

Zeller, B. (2022). *How Many Died in the American Civil War?* history.com.

One Last Addition

If you dream of leaving a legacy, achieve your dreams without delay. Today is the perfect time to accomplish something amazing. You have the opportunity right now to make an impact on the world. Even if that impact appears small in the beginning, I urge you to begin at this very moment. Drop what you are doing and put in writing your legacy goals. Then put into writing on how you might achieve them. There is no time to spare.

I had spent more than a couple years thinking about writing this book, before I actually sat down and began the process. A mirid of obstacles always seemed to prevail. Life in general got in the way.

Eventually I took a personal and honest inventory of the utilization of my time. It then became obvious that the sheer importance of my legacy meant more to me than the excuses I was making to myself, and I started making a concentrated effort to write this book.

From there I worked on this project every chance I could, creating time slots in my life by eliminating things that were less important.

A mere six hours after proudly announcing to my fiancé that I had finally finished this book, I found myself in an ambulance being rushed to the hospital. My heart rate had shot up without warning to 230 beats per minute and I was in danger of cardiac arrest. The cardiology team put me under sedation and used shock paddles to perform a rebooting of my heart. While I am much better now, my life could have easily ended before I was able to push the publish button on my legacy.

"To leave a legacy, you must first make a commitment to your dreams."

-Rory Curtis

Made in United States
Orlando, FL
18 August 2023